FOREWORD

The present law provides that the unsworn evidence of any child under the age of fourteen must be corroborated. This provision is based on the assumption that, if the child cannot take the oath, his or her evidence is inherently too unreliable to form the sole basis for a conviction. The purpose of the following review is to examine research studies which have focused on the reliability of children's evidence in order to discover whether this assumption is justified.

MARY TUCK

Head of the Research and Planning Unit

ACKNOWLEDGEMENTS

I would like to thank Professor Graham Davies for suggesting a number of very helpful references and Dr. Jonquil Drinkwater for allowing me to see manuscript copies of the papers which are to be published as The Child Witness: Do the Courts abuse Children?

CAROL HEDDERMAN

CHILDREN'S EVIDENCE: THE NEED FOR CORROBORATION

Carol Hedderman

RESEARCH AND PLANNING UNIT PAPER 41

London: Home Office

RESEARCH AND PLANNING UNIT PAPERS

'Research and Planning Unit Papers' contain material of a rather more specialised nature than that which appears in the Unit's main publication outlet, the Home Office Research Studies series. As with that series, they result from research undertaken in the Home Office to assist in the exercise of its administrative functions, and for the information of the judicature, the services for which the Home Secretary has responsibility (direct or indirect), and the general public.

On the last pages of this paper are listed titles already published in this series (the first four titles were known as Research Unit Papers) in the Home Office Research Studies series and in the earlier series Studies in the Causes of Delinquency and the Treatment of Offenders.

ISBN 0 86252 304 4
ISSN 0262 1738

ii

CONTENTS

1. INTRODUCTION

The belief that children do not make competent witnesses was embodied in early canon law which stated that anyone beneath the age of puberty should be barred from giving evidence in the ecclesiastical courts. Doubts concerning the reliability of children's evidence were also apparent in the rules of evidence pertaining to English common law. The testimony of children at or over the age of seven might be admitted if the court was satisfied that he or she understood the oath. Children under this age, however, were excluded from giving evidence on the grounds that they were not capable of understanding the meaning or significance of giving sworn testimony (Goodman, 1984).

In Rex v. Braiser (1779) it was acknowledged that admitting or excluding a child's evidence solely on the basis of age was an unsatisfactory way of distinguishing between those who were capable of giving evidence and those who were not. From this time judges have been empowered to determine a child's competence to give sworn testimony by questioning the child to ensure that he or she understood the significance of the oath.

According to Section 38 of the Children and Young Person's Act 1933, if any child under the age of 14 is considered incapable of giving sworn testimony his or her evidence may still may admissible; however, unsworn testimony must be independently corroborated. In reality, the distinction between sworn and unsworn testimony, as Spencer (1987:243) has pointed out is now "a distinction without difference." Understanding the nature of the oath used to mean that the child believed he or she would go to hell for lying; now it simply means that the child appreciates the solemnity of the occasion and recognises the importance of telling the truth.

It is of course essential that <u>all</u> the evidence which is presented to a court in any criminal cases meets certain basic standards of veracity and reliability. The sexual abuse of children is regarded as a particularly heinous crime which merits severe legal and social censure and it is reasonable that the rules of evidence should be enforced stringently in such cases to ensure that no innocent defendant is wrongly convicted. However, it is not self-evident that this should be achieved by embodying the presumption in the law that children are prone to lie, fantasise or misremember and by insisting that their unsworn testimony is accompanied by independent corroboration.

2. SEXUAL ABUSE

The circumstances in which crimes of sexual abuse are committed often mean that the young victim of the offence is also the only witness to it. If other adults witness abuse they are often unwilling to testify either because of their relationship to the defendant or because of their involvement in the offence. If other children witness the abuse their evidence is often excluded because one unsworn witness may not corroborate the evidence of another. Independent physical evidence of abuse may not exist (Krugman and Jones, 1987): it is possible that fewer than one in three victims of sexual abuse display any physical symptoms (Mann, 1985). Moreover, certain physical signs which may have been caused by sexual abuse may also be attributable to natural physical disorders. For example, it is not always easy to distinguish between the tissue damage caused by anal intercourse and that caused by constipation in young children.

3. WHY DOUBT CHILDREN'S EVIDENCE?

Casting doubts on the veracity or capacity of the child witness is a questionable way of protecting the falsely accused offender: it may well be based on false assumptions concerning the prevalence of child abuse and the reasons children withdraw allegations of abuse.

Practitioners' estimates and self-report studies indicate that the sexual abuse of children is far more prevalent than the official figures suggest (McCord, 1986). It is likely that at least 8% of girls and 3% of boys in the U.S. are abused. The limited information available suggests that children in Britain are equally vulnerable. A survey by MORI (1984) found that 10% of their sample of 2,019 adults had experienced some form of sexual abuse before the age of sixteen. These figures, however, included reports of non-contact abuse such as indecent exposure. In Nash and West's (1985) study six hundred women were questioned about sexual abuse. On the basis of their findings, and allowing for a high non-response rate of around 58%, the authors concluded that at least 16% of women in Britain were likely to have experienced sexual abuse involving physical contact before the age of sixteen. In over 50% of the cases in the sample the offender was known to the victim and in a third of these cases the abuser and the victim were related. In America, it is estimated that between 50% and 80% of victims know their abusers and in 24% to 50% of cases they are related (McCord, 1986).

In only half of the cases included in Nash and West's sample did the victim tell anyone about abusive experiences and less than a fifth (17%) of cases were reported to the police. Similar levels of under-reporting have been discovered in America (eg Corsini-Munt, 1982). Despite the high level of under-reporting associated with sexual abuse, it is often assumed that many accusations of abuse are false. There appear to be a number of reasons for this impression. First, children in general are thought to lie more frequently than adults and to be unable to distinguish fact from fantasy. Secondly, and relatedly, these stereotypical assumptions have been given greater credibility in relation to children who claim to be abused by reference to Freud (1959) who interpreted the fact that so many of his female patients reported being abused as children as examples of childhood fantasies. Thirdly, the fact that some children withdraw sexual abuse allegations is assumed to mean: a) that these allegations were false; and b) that some of those who persist in their allegations are lying. However, none of these factors, individually or collectively, provide a sound basis for generally doubting children's testimony.

Children in general may or may not lie more than adults, but this is no reason to doubt the testimony of the individual child. As a government committee in Canada recently reported (Committee on Sexual Offences against Children and Youths, 1984:372):

> "The Committees's research findings indicate that conventional assumptions about the veracity and powers of recall of young children are largely unfounded and, in any event, vary significantly among different children, as they do among adults".

It is quite possible that children are thought to lie more frequently than adults because they are more frequently detected in doing so (Feldman *et al.*, 1979).

Freud's belief that his patients had not really experienced abuse was not based on empirical evidence but on his refusal to believe that abuse was as prevalent as his patients' claims would suggest. Children do fantasise and there is evidence which suggests that they are not always able to distinguish between what they have done and what they only thought of doing (Johnson and Foley, 1984). However, there is no evidence that this deficiency in their discriminatory abilities extends to the actions of others or that such a finding is true for tasks and conditions which occur outside the laboratory. Also, there is no obvious reason why children should fantasise about sexual abuse. Moreover, the descriptions of sexual activities furnished by abused children are qualitatively different to those made by children who have learnt about sex at second hand through films or as passive observers of adults (Conerly, 1986; McCord, 1986). It has also been suggested that children who have been abused play with anatomically correct dolls in a different way to those who have not experienced abuse (Glazer, 1986), although this has been disputed[1].

Lastly, children do not necessarily withdraw abuse allegations because they are untrue. Most legal, medical and social work practitioners

---

[1] King and Yuille (1987) have argued that anatomically correct dolls suggest a play pattern to children which may be misinterpreted as evidence of abuse. However, they do not present any evidence to support this claim.

accept that children may withdraw an accusation either because they are afraid of being attacked again (Berliner and Barbieri, 1984) or, when the abuser is a family member, they are worried about the consequences of official intervention for themselves and their family (Weiss, 1983). One American psychiatrist has estimated that fewer than 2% of children who allege that they have been abused are lying (Mann, 1985) and the results of a recent study appear to confirm this (Jones and McGraw, 1987). Other practitioners have said that many of the children who report abuse under-report the amount and type of abuse (Berliner and Barbieri, 1984). Unfortunately, reliable information about the proportion of children who withdraw allegations is not available, nor do we know at what stage of official proceedings an allegation is likely to be withdrawn.

4. EMPIRICAL RESEARCH

If, as has been suggested, there are no *a priori* reasons for assuming that children are unreliable and untrustworthy witnesses, there is also no *a priori* reason for insisting that the unsworn testimony of children should be independently corroborated. Indeed, the Criminal Law Revision Committee (1972) recommended that the corroboration requirement should be dispensed with in non-sexual cases. However, the Committee also recommended that the corroboration requirement should be maintained in relation to the evidence of the alleged victims of sexual abuse on the grounds that under the age of fourteen children's poor memories make them unreliable witnesses.

Given the fact that independent corroboration is extremely unlikely to be available in cases of sexual abuse there may be very good reasons for wishing to dispense with such a requirement. The need for independent corroboration should be determined on the basis of what we know about child witnesses and not what is assumed about them. The remainder of this review, therefore, is devoted to critically examining empirical studies which have investigated children's memory and suggestibility; the extent to which different interview techniques affect the amount and accuracy of children's descriptions of people and events; the extent to which children lie or confuse fact with fantasy; and the extent to which adults regard the evidence of children as credible. Particular attention is given throughout the review to the methods which were used in each of the studies described in order to consider the extent to which their findings are relevant to the courtroom.

The objectives of this review are to discover:

i) whether any evidence exists which either supports or refutes the view that children do not make competent witnesses;

ii) whether particular interview techniques produce more, and more accurate, information than others;

iii) whether age limits have been identified below which children's evidence should be regarded with suspicion; and

iv) whether, when children appear as witnesses in court, their evidence is believed.

Finally, the use of video technology is considered to see whether the use of video links and video recordings would exacerbate or alleviate the problems associated with obtaining and using the evidence of children.

Memory and Susceptibility to Suggestion

Three related aspects of memory research are of interest in considering whether children make reliable witnesses. These concern accuracy of recall and recognition, suggestibility, and the capacity to distinguish between what subjects remember thinking and what they remember experiencing.

The process whereby information is stored and retrieved is commonly held to consist of three distinct stages (Loftus, 1979). In the first stage (acquisition) information is perceived and encoded. In the second stage (retention) information is stored subsequent to the event and prior to the third stage (retrieval) at which stored information is accessed. Memory can breakdown or be altered at any one of these stages (Rabinowitz, 1985).

Research which has focused on adults has concluded that their powers of recall and recognition are poor and that they are susceptible to suggestion (Jenkins and Davies, 1985; Loftus, 1979; Loftus and Green, 1980; Gorenstein and Ellsworth, 1980). Studies which have concentrated exclusively on children have come to very similar conclusions (Dale et al., 1978; Johnson and Foley, 1984). Unfortunately, very few studies have compared adults and children in either respect. Also, those comparative studies which do exist have produced conflicting results. Although contradictory findings may be a consequence of methodological differences and imperfections (Malpass and Devine, 1981), this lack of agreement also suggests that memory is not simply a function of age.

In a study by Marin et al. (1979) ninety-six subjects aged between 5 and 25 years of age were compared on their ability to recall details of a staged incident a) by free recall, b) in response to a series of questions of which one was (mis)leading, and c) to identify one of the actors involved in the incident from photographs. Marin and her colleagues found that both children and adults were lamentably poor eyewitnesses. Subjects recalled less than a fifth of the items they could have recalled and gave incorrect answers to 25% of the objective questions. Twenty-five per cent of subjects were also misled by leading questions and almost 50% could not recognise the man they had just seen from photographs. The authors concluded that although young children were less capable of providing free narrative descriptions of what they had observed, they were as accurate as adults in answering objective questions and identifying the actor from photographs. There was no evidence of an age difference in the subjects susceptibility to leading questions. Five year olds were no less competent or reliable as eyewitnesses than adults when responding to direct and objective questions. Also, although the five year olds were less capable of providing a narrative description of what they had observed, what they did say tended to be correct.

The fact that Marin *et al.* found no age-related differences may well be related to the study's methodological shortcomings. Yarmey (1984), for example, criticised Marin and her colleagues for only asking one leading question and for their failure to report omission rates. However, the study was more realistic than many of the other studies of children's memory which have been conducted as these have often used word lists (Eysenck and Baron, 1974), pictures (Brown and Campione, 1972) or filmed incidents (Cohen and Harnick, 1980) to test recall rather than staging live events. It also used a comparatively large sample[2]. Indeed, the main reason for doubting the generalisability of Marin at al.'s findings lies in the fact that most of the other researchers in this field have concluded that the ability

----

[2] Eysenck and Brown (1974) examined the cued and uncued recall of 2 groups of 36 children aged five and eight. Brown and Campione (1972) tested a total of 51 pre-school children in three experiments and Cohen and Harnick (1980) compared the recall abilities of 36 subjects.

to recall and recognise stimuli, and vulnerability to suggestion, are connected to, if not entirely dependent on, age (Jablonski, 1974; Cohen and Harnick, 1980; Dale *et al.*, 1978; Goodman and Reed, 1986).

The study by Goodman and Reed (1986) is particularly interesting and pertinent to a debate about child witnesses in cases of sexual abuse, because it is one of the few which has examined age differences in the eyewitness testimony of participants in an incident rather than just that of bystanders. It was also one of the few which has tested nondeliberate memory and thus, may be regarded as a comparatively realistic experiment.

In Goodman and Reed's study 32 children aged 3 and 6 and 16 adults were asked both objective and suggestive questions about their interaction with an unfamiliar adult in an incident which lasted 5 minutes. They were also asked to identify the experimenters' confederate from a series of photographs. The authors concluded that the adults and the six year olds did not differ in their ability to answer objective questions or to identify the confederate. The six year olds were however more susceptible to suggestion and they recalled less about the incident than the adults. The three-year olds answered fewer objective questions than the older subjects. They also recalled less, identified confederates less frequently and were the most susceptible to suggestion[3].

In contrast to Goodman and Reed's finding that adults and six-year old children were similar in their abilities to recognise the confederate, Chance and Goldstein (1984) say that children under twelve years of age do less well on facial recognition tests. However, the studies on which they base this opinion were not realistic analogues of witnessing as they involved the presentation of single view photographs of sets of faces for subsequent recognition.

Other recent studies which have used videotaped or live incidents have found, like Goodman and Reed, that there are minimal age effects on children's ability to make identifications from photographs (eg. Parker *et al.*, 1986). However, as Davies and Flin (1987b) have pointed out, these results come from studies in which the target face was always present in the photographic array. Age differences have been found in experiments which have examined children's performance when the target face was absent from the array. For example, in the study by Yuille *et al.* (1986) when the performance of children aged 8 to 9, 10 to 11 and 12 to 14 were compared, the youngest

---

[3] In an even more realistic study, Goodman used a naturally occurring (and stressful) event to examine children's nondeliberate memory and susceptibility to suggestion (see Goodman *et al.*, 1987b). Suggestive questioning produced incorrect answers about the room in which the incident had taken place, but children as young as three years old resisted suggestion concerning the physical characteristics of the adult with whom they interacted. Although 3 and 4 year olds did make more false identifications from photographs than older children, the difference was not statistically significant. This study provides useful information about the ability of young children to act as witnesses, but it does not show how they compare with adults. Also, the oldest subjects in the sample of 48 were six years old.

children were found to be especially likely to select the wrong photograph, rather than refusing to make a selection. In real life, as Davies and Flin suggest, holding both offender present and offender absent parades would reveal when young children make this type of error. Indeed, this has already been done in America to check the identification evidence of a three year old child (Jones, 1987).

Cohen and Harnick (1980) compared 8 and 11 year old children with college students on their ability to recall events from a film in the face of misleading questions from an interrogator. There were twelve subjects in each of the three age groups. Initial tests showed that the eleven year olds were comparable to the college students in terms of their powers of recall and their ability to resist suggestion. Six year olds were inferior to the other two groups in both respects. However, when a second test was carried out a week later, there were no significant differences between the two groups in the extent to which erroneous information had been incorporated into memory.

Cohen and Harnick realised that their results might have been affected by some (older) subjects realising that they were being given false suggestions, but they claimed that this would maximise intergroup differences even if it decreased the magnitude of the suggestibility effect on the results of the second session. Moreover, the study by Yuille *et al.* (1986) achieved similar results to Cohen and Harnick when they discovered that although children conformed to a misleading suggestion in an initial interview, they did not carry erroneous information forward to a later test of recall. These results fit the suggestion that the children were responding to a desire to be seen as socially conforming rather than displaying cognitive malleability

(Davies and Flin, 1987a). However, a study by Loftus and Palmer (1974) and the work by Weinberg *et al.* (1983) with adults suggests that simple compliance to demand pressure does not fully explain altered recollections.

Children's susceptibility to suggestion may depend on the degree of linguistic competence which is required to comprehend the suggestion (Johnson and Foley, 1984; Loftus and Davies, 1984). Unfortunately, no studies appear to have investigated this claim directly. However, there is evidence that performance on memory tests and vulnerabilty to (mis)leading questions are related to knowledge (Chi, 1978), to stress (Dent, 1977; Dent and Stephenson, 1979a; Pynoos and Eth, 1984) and to the interrogatory style used to elicit information (Dent and Stephenson, 1979b; Dent, 1982). Two recent studies (Yuille *et al.*, 1986; Goodman *et al.*, 1987b) have also provided evidence to support the claim that children's susceptibility to suggestion may depend on the extent to which the stimuli are important or interesting to them (Loftus and Davies, 1984). Finally, there is some evidence to support Brown's (1975) contention that intelligence and memory are related for children (Feinman and Entwhistle, 1976; Goldstein and Chance, 1964) if not for adults (Chance and Goldstein, 1984).

On balance, the available evidence does not support the view that memory and resistance to suggestion are a function of age. If they were, performance would be more uniform across different conditions and different tasks for particular age groups. However, the available evidence does support the view that accuracy and reliability of recall are related to a certain level of cognitive maturity (Brown, 1975; Davies, 1980; Chance and Goldstein, 1984). In other words, age-related improvements on memory performance tasks are associated with the ability to think conceptually rather than in purely concrete terms; an increasing repetoire of concepts; and a greater understanding of how and when to extrapolate from one situation to another. The extent to which this is relevant to children's ability to act as witnesses depends on how, and under what conditions, this relationship operates.

An increasing number of psychologists now believe that age-related improvements in memory reflect the acquisition (Ornstein, 1978) and orchestration (Jablonski, 1974) of techniques for operating the memory system. They are not simply the result of an organic process whereby structural aspects of memory undergo developmental changes as children grow older (Kail, 1985): the change is more accurately regarded as one of refinement (Davies, 1980).

Brown (1975) claims that this more sophisticated model holds true for both "strategic" (deliberate) and "non-strategic" (nondeliberate) memory. In a later article Brown (1982) says that both learning and retrieval strategies undergo rapid development between the ages of five and ten. However, she also says that there is no reason to believe that children take in (mediation) fewer details as a result of their cognitve immaturity, unless this means that the stimuli are too complex or sophisticated to be within their comprehension. Also, the impact of learning strategies on performance will be minimised when the test involves nondeliberate memory (Davies *et al.*, 1986); although a meaningful structure is required to retrieve information (production) which has been acquired strategically or non-strategically (Brown, 1975). This theory has obvious implications for the way child witnesses are perceived and handled.

The victims of child abuse, and many other forms of crime, rarely exercise deliberate memory skills at the time of the offence. However, they are commonly required to exercise deliberate production skills to recall details of the event and, in some cases, to identify an attacker. If nondeliberate memory mediation depended on the development of sophisticated techniques, children under 10 might be immutably unreliable witnesses. If, however, such techniques are only required at the production stage, the problem is one of access and not availability (Tulving, 1983).

Interview Techniques

Several studies have been carried out to discover whether it is possible to enhance recognition and recall in children by providing external prompts and cues which alleviate or overcome production deficiency.

Jablonski (1974) has argued that children as young as five years of age do better on tests of their recall abilities when they are prompted. The study by Davies and Brown (1978) provides support for the view that young children suffer from production rather than mediation deficiency and that cueing aids recall. In this study the actual and potential strategies available to a group of 48 five year old children were tested by varying the conditions of recall and presentation of 20 objects drawn from 5 different categories. Information was presented either randomly or in blocks and recall was cued and uncued. Both the manner in which the information was presented and the manner in which it was elicited had an overall effect, with blocked presentation and cued recall enhancing the number of items recalled. However, blocking only affected within—category recall, whereas cueing affected the number of categories recalled. An earlier study by Eysenck and Baron (1974) which examined the effects of cueing on the recall of categorised word lists had reached very similar conclusions.

Once again, however, it should be noted that there is not complete agreement between different researchers concerning the benefits of prompted recall. Dent and Stephenson's (1979b) study of the ability of children aged 10 and 11 to recall events from a film of a theft, did not find that asking either general or specific questions enhanced recall accuracy, although asking questions did elicit more information. Also, the results of a later, more realistic study by one of the authors (Dent, 1982:295), which examined the questioning styles of 6 experienced and 6 inexperienced interviewers, persuaded her that although unprompted descriptive recall is still the most accurate:

> "...it appears that general questions can be used to obtain further information without detriment to accuracy, provided no pressure is put on the child to give an answer".

The study by Dale *et al.* (1978) focused specifically on the way objective and leading questions affected the testimony of preschool children. Thirty—two boys and girls aged between 4 years, 2 months and 5 years, 6 months were questioned after they had seen a series of

48 short films. The study showed that the form of the question did not significantly alter the answers to questions which were present in the films; however, it did have an effect on the answers to questions about anything which was not in the film. This research is particularly interesting because it helps to show the type of questions which are misleading. For example, the question "Did you see a....." produced more correct answers than the question "Did you see the.....".

In a much earlier study, Stern (1910) compared the accounts of subjects aged 7, 11, 13, 16, and 18 which were produced under free recall conditions and in response to leading questions in cross-examination. He found that leading questions resulted in an average error score of between 25% and 30%, whereas the average error rate associated with free recall was between 5% and 10%. He also found that the accuracy of the younger children's accounts was particularly badly affected.

Finally, Berliner and Barbieri (1984) have even suggested that children as young as three can give accurate and truthful accounts in response to objective questioning which takes account of children's cognitive immaturity. However, aside from a single, rather small study by Nelson (1978), this opinion was not based on any form of controlled study but on the authors' experiences as sexual abuse therapists. Moreover, the recent study by Goodman *et al.* (1987b) showed that the 3 and 4 year olds in their sample were significantly less likely than the 5 and 6 year olds to answer objective questions correctly. Also, although most of the mistakes made by both age groups in response to objective questions were errors of omission

(98%), it is worth noting that all of the errors of commission were made by the younger children.

Fantasies and Fabrication

Over the course of four different experiments, Johnson and Foley (1984) examined the hypothesis that children might be less reliable witnesses than adults because of their inability to distinguish between what they had said, seen, heard or done, and what they had only thought. They found that children as young as six years old were as capable as older subjects of distinguishing between internal (imagined) and external (perceived) classes of experience. For example, they could distinguish between imagined and perceived words and imagined and perceived pictures. The only task on which both six and nine year old subjects performed less well than adults was in distinguishing between the actions they had carried out and those they had only imagined doing. However, it may be unwise to extrapolate from these findings to claim that children who allege abuse may confuse actual events and situations they only imagined.

The confidence with which it is possible to generalise from experimental findings is partly determined by the size of the sample and by its representativeness. Unfortunately, Johnson and Foley do not provide any information about their samples, aside from specifying the age groups they tested. Thus, it may be unwise to assume that their results hold for anyone other than those in the samples. Also, the unsophisticated stimuli used in these experiments bear no relation to the complex information children who allege abuse would be asked to provide in courtroom testimony. Moreover, as the authors point out, this study considered whether children confused their own actions with imagined actions. They did not consider whether children confuse other people's actions with what they imagine other people have done. Finally, Johnson and Foley's experiments involved instructing subjects to deliberately imagine an event. This may well have resulted in the generation of fantasies which were qualitatively different to those which occur spontaneously[4].

The question of whether children do lie more than adults cannot be answered from existing empirical evidence. There appears to be virtually no evidence on children's moral ability or propensity to tell the truth. However, many psychiatrists and therapists who work with abused children believe that far from fabricating or exaggerating incidents of abuse children conceal and under-report such experiences (eg. Berliner and Barbieri, 1984; Mann, 1985).

One group of Freudian psychiatrists (Rosenfeld *et al.*, 1979) do claim that allegations of abuse made by children under the age of nine should be carefully scrutinised. They say that children aged eight or less are often less able to distinguish between fantasy and reality than older children. However, they also say that only a very small minority of children fantasise about abuse and they claim that by

---

[4] In fairness, it should be said that not only does Johnson now recognise the limitations of these studies, but she is carrying out a new series of more realistic and sophisticated experiments designed to examine children's ability to distinguish between memories of naturally occurring events and spontaneous fantasies (see Linsay and Johnson, 1987). Unfortunately the results of these experiments are not yet available.

asking a series of questions relating to the child's mental history and family background it is usually possible to distinguish between real and false accounts. Rosenfeld and his colleagues also suggest that some young children may have been abused but that they misidentify their attackers. This last point has also been made by other psychiatrists (eg. Goodwin *et al.*, 1980).

Aside from the anecdotal and impressionistic accounts provided by practitioners, the only evidence which appears to be available on the extent to which children fabricate accusations of abuse are the results of a recent American study (Jones and McGraw, 1987). In this research all the (516) reports of child sexual abuse made to the Denver Department of Social Services in 1983 were examined. In 137 cases there was insufficient evidence to judge whether abuse had taken place. Of the remaining 439 reports, 34 (7.7%) were judged to be fictitious. In only 8 cases were the fictions generated by children and four of the five children who made these accusations had prior histories of sexual abuse. In considering these results it should be remembered that the researchers did not have an absolutely reliable test of the occurrence of child abuse. An allegation was judged to be true or false according to clinical criteria, such as, the degree of explicit detail a child's statement contained, the child's psychological response to the abusive incident, his or her family history, and so on. Any claims made by the child which could be independently verified, such as the presence of others during the abuse, were checked and an assessment was made as to whether the incident could have taken place at the time and place described in the allegation. The use of these different criteria ensured that no allegation was judged to be false on the basis of a single dubious factor, however, it is still possible that the clinical judgement was incorrect.

Feldman and his associates (1979) examined the extent to which adults were able to detect deception via facial expressions in 6, 13, and 19 year old males and females. Untrained judges showed greater accuracy in decoding whether six year olds were lying or telling the truth than when they tried to gauge the veracity of the older age groups. The researchers suggested that this may be due to the greater cognitive maturity of the older children and their greater ability to consciously control non-verbal behaviour. Another study by Feldman and White (1980) examined the extent to which both body language and facial expressions enabled untrained judges to spot deception. In this study 74 boys and girls aged between 5 and 12 were asked to lie about their preferences for two drinks. Once again, older children were better at concealing a lie. Interestingly, this study also found gender differences in the way both younger and older children concealed deception. Girls in the older two groups revealed more through their body language, whereas younger girls revealed more thorough their facial expressions. Older boys gave more away through facial expressions.

On the basis of these two studies, it seems that if any children are to be distrusted it is older rather than younger ones as older children are more able to deceive. However, it might be unwise to generalise from these findings given that both studies employed highly artificial scenarios and used an issue in which the "deceivers" were unlikely to have any investment or interest. Once again, the absence of more realistic studies makes definitive statements about being able to judge when children are lying about abuse impossible. Furthermore, these studies do not say anything about the relative propensity of different age groups to lie.

One way of identifying false accusations of abuse may be to employ polygraph (lie detection) tests. McCord (1986) mentions that one hundred and forty-seven children who claimed that they had been sexually abused were referred to a polygraph examiner by the Michigan police over the course of a 5 year period (1969-1974). Only one child was judged to have made a false allegation. Unfortunately, McCord does not say how old the children were, why the police chose to refer them to the polygraph examiner or what proportion of the total number of children who made allegations of sexual abuse these 147 children represented. Also, although proponents of this method argue that lie detection tests are becoming increasingly accurate and reliable (Gudjonsonn, 1983), evidence of this is scant. Moreover, it is arguable that the use of such tests on children is inappropriate because they may be too stressful. If polygraph examinations are to be considered seriously as a means of detecting false allegations of abuse, the advantages and problems which are said to be associated with such tests must be investigated empirically. Such research should include a consideration of the particular circumstances and problems of abused children.

"Statement Reality Analysis" is another method which has been advocated as an aid to judging the veracity of children's allegations of abuse in Britain. This method is already employed in Germany by some psychologists when they are asked to advise a court on the reliability of child witnesses. This method is based on the assumption that unfounded or distorted accounts <u>are</u> discernably different from those which truthfully represent reality (Undeutsch, 1982). Unfortunately, this assumption does not appear to have been tested and current statement reality analysis criteria are acknowledged even by its supporters to be in need of refinement (Kohnken and Steller, 1987).

Credibility

Goodman and her colleagues (1987a) examined the hypothesis that irrespective of whether or not children's reputation as poor witnesses was justified, jurors reacted to them as less credible than their adult counterparts. Over three separate tests, jurors were more willing to believe the testimony of adult witnesses. However, the authors say that these results might not hold when the child witness was also a victim. They point out that in sexual abuse cases younger children might be perceived as <u>more</u> credible than older ones when their age precludes them from having legitimate sexual experiences. Unfortunately this hypothesis has not been examined directly. However, the results of another recent study of the way mock jurors react to child witnesses offer some support for this suggestion.

Ross *et al*. (1987) examined the way 50 mock jurors responded to the same evidence when it was given by witnesses aged 8, 21 or 74 in a videotaped trial. Jurors were found to view the child witness more positively than the young adult or elderly witness. The authors suggest that this was because the jurors had lower expectations concerning the child witness's ability to give evidence. Thus, when a detailed description of a fairly complex event was given by a child the jurors were impressed, whereas they would have expected this sort of description from an adult. However, it is worth noting that, whilst the young and elderly witnesses' credibility ratings were associated with the final decision concerning the defendant's guilt, the credibility of the child witness was not. It would seem that in making this decision the jurors tended to discount the child witness's testimony and rely on other evidence.

Finally, as Goodman *et al.* (1987a) and Ross *et al.* (1987) acknowledge, their studies were not realistic analogues of actual trials. Experiments such as these are useful for theory testing and for defining empirical hypotheses to be tested in larger, more sophisticated simulations and in archival and field research. However, it may be unwise to extrapolate from such experiments to the courtroom.

5. CONCLUSIONS

Do children make competent witnesses?

There is virtually no evidence available on which to judge whether children are prone to fantasise or lie about abuse. With the single exception of the study by Jones and McGraw (1987), the only evidence there is consists primarily of case histories and psychiatrists' anecdotes and is rarely based on a consideration of more than half a dozen cases. This question really needs much more rigorous and thorough investigation.

There is some, very limited, evidence that children of six and eight confuse what they have done with what they have only thought of doing. However, there is not enough information available on the size and characteristics of the samples used in the studies which reached these conclusions to generalise from their findings to abused children. Also, the question of whether children confuse what other people have done with what they have only imagined them doing has not been investigated.

Memory capacity does not appear to be a function of age. However, the acquisition and orchestration of techniques for operating the memory system appear to be related to other forms of cognitive maturation, such as the ability to think conceptually. Estimates of the age at which children begin to think conceptually vary between five and seven. Twelve year old children do not appear to perform differently from adults on any form of memory test.

Nondeliberate memory is clearly less reliant on the use of sophisticated operational techniques than deliberate memory and the availability of these techniques seems to have a greater effect on the ability to retrieve information than the ability to acquire it. Children who are the victims of sexual abuse do not usually exercise deliberate memory skills at the time of the offence. In other words, they rarely attempt to deliberately memorise details of the incident or identifying information about the assailant. However, they are required to exercise deliberate recall and recognition techniques when acting as witnesses in legal contexts. Thus, whilst children even younger than five may have stored some information about an abusive experience, the question of whether they can be reliable witnesses depends on whether their memories are robust and whether it is possible to compensate for their lack of deliberate recall skills by external cues.

The results of all the studies which have investigated the suggestibility of adults and children show that people of all ages are prone to suggestion and that at least some erroneous information is usually carried forward into future descriptions of individuals or events. There is also general, though not complete, agreement that children under five are particularly vulnerable to suggestion. It is reasonable to conclude from this that although children as young as three may be able to give accurate and truthful accounts in response to objective questioning which takes account of their cognitive immaturity, it would be unwise to rely on such evidence alone. By the time a case comes to court a young child's memory may have faded. It may also have become confused or distorted by earlier suggestive questioning. Perhaps even more importantly, involving children under five years of age in legal proceedings and encouraging them to retain memories of an offence may also add to the psychological damage caused by the abuse (Pynoos and Eth, 1984). Of course, this may also be true for much older children and adults, but it is particularly difficult to justify given that the evidentiary value of very young children's evidence is doubtful.

Interview Techniques

The studies which have compared the benefits and disadvantages of different interview techniques have found that asking children and adults leading questions undermines rather than enhances the accuracy and reliability of their evidence. Asking children nonleading questions will result in more information being recalled. Objective questioning may also enhance the accuracy of recall in children, although the evidence is not unequivocal.

At least two of the practitioners who work with abused children believe that even leading questions can help to elicit accurate and detailed accounts of abuse. Bentovim and Tranter (1987) acknowledge that suggestive questions may encourage a child to say what he or she thinks a questioner wants to hear. However, they also make the point that, in interviewing children who may have been abused, they are hypothesis testing. Unlike experimenters who know the correct answers to the questions they ask, the therapist may have little idea what the correct answers are to their questions. The problem with this idea is, as Tschirgi (1980) has shown, that when people try to test hypotheses they preferentially search for evidence which will support those hypotheses! With the possible exception of Dent (1982), Bentovim and Tranter's complaints concerning the lack of realism in studies of interviewing techniques do seem to be justified. More experiments are needed which closely replicate real-life conditions.

The impact of stress on memory acquisition has recently been investigated using naturally stressful events, such as a visit to the dentist (Peters, 1987) or an inoculation clinic (Goodman *et al.*, 1987b). Given the ethical problems associated with using abused children in experiments (Melton, 1981), it might be useful to adopt similar procedures to investigate the impact of stress and other factors on recall and recognition.

Bentovim and Tranter (1987) make a second, interesting point about objective questioning. They claim that it does not help them to overcome the resistance many abused children feel towards speaking about their experiences. Although they do not appear to appreciate that the use of anatomically correct dolls may result in nonverbal suggestion, they do admit that the suggestive interviewing style they developed as a clinical technique must be modified if their interviews are to be videotaped and used as evidence in the courts. The authors and their colleagues at Great Ormond Street Hospital are currently investigating the impact of a new more objective (verbal) style by looking at its utility in cases where there is other evidence of abuse, such as clear and consistent medical evidence. Real-life research of this sort is obviously highly desirable both in its own right and as a criterion for assessing the generalisability of experimental results.

Age Limits

Although English law does not debar a child from giving evidence on the grounds of age, it is very exceptional for a child under the age of five to be allowed to testify. The results of the studies discussed in this review suggest that this practice is generally sound. However, individual children of three or four may be capable of giving accurate and reasonably full evidence in response to objective questioning if they have been shielded from suggestive questioning at earlier examinations.

It may be true, as Rosenfeld *et al*. (1979) suggest, that children under the age of nine are not always able to distinguish fact and fantasy, but their accounts of imagined and real events appear to be sufficently dissimilar for this to be apparent. Also, concentrating on the extent to which younger children fantasise and fabricate may be misplaced as older children seem to be better at dissembling. Unfortunately, the question of whether the propensity to lie is age related does not appear to have been investigated. Nor does there appear to have been any research into age differences in the moral ability to tell the truth. Thus, there is no evidence to show whether the current legislative distinction between witnesses above and below the age of fourteen is valid.

Overall, it might be preferable to seek the advice of child psychologists and psychiatrists and to investigate other techniques for assessing veracity, such as Statement Reality Analysis, rather than issuing general warnings about the testimony of whole age groups when the police or courts suspect that an individual child is lying or has confused actual and imagined events.

Credibility

When children give uncorroborated evidence in any sort of criminal case Crown Court judges are obliged to warn jurors of the dangers of convicting anyone on such evidence. The question of whether jurors follow such advice does not appear to have been investigated in this country. One of the few American studies which examined the extent to which children are regarded as credible witnesses found that in three separate experiments mock jurors were more willing to believe the testimony of adults. In all three experiments the witness was a bystander not a victim and the crime was one of vehicular homicide, not sexual abuse. Thus, it may may be unwise to extrapolate from these findings to claim that jurors in this country are likely to disbelieve children who allege that they have been sexually abused. Also, in another similar study, mock jurors appeared more willing to believe a child than a young adult or elderly witness. However, the jurors also tended to discount the childs evidence in deciding whether to convict the defendant. In the light of such findings, admonishing jurors to view children's evidence sceptically seems a somewhat dubious exercise. There is no proof that the evidence of any child of five or more is unreliable. In addition, jurors may already be biased against such witnesses and, even if child witnesses are believed, their testimony may still be discounted.

Video Technology

If the general tenor of existing research is to be believed the advent of video links would have the advantage of reducing the debilitating effect of stress on the child's memory by removing the child from the courtroom. The desirability of video recordings is less certain. One advantage of admitting video evidence is that it provides an account which, if secured soon after disclosure, will be freshest and least tainted by subsequent discussions and interrogations (Jones, 1987). Indeed, this was one consideration behind the recent move by the Legislature in South Australia to allow video evidence to be used in committal proceedings and as part of the main trial.

It would also be less traumatic for the child if the number of times he or she had to repeat the details of an abusive incident was reduced. However, this would depend on a high level of inter-agency co-operation which only currently exists in Bexley and a few other areas (Gwynn, 1987). This development might also limit the extent to which a defendant can exercise the right to cross-examine witnesses. Again this is an area which would benefit from further investigation via real-life, or at least more realistic, experimentation.

6.0 THE NEED FOR CORROBORATION

The extent to which it is possible to extrapolate from the findings of existing research to the evidence of the young victims of sexual abuse is doubtful. Virtually all of the studies discussed in this review used samples of less than a hundred and most were based on samples of less than fifty. Also, information about the ethnic and class composition of the samples was rarely provided so it not possible to judge how representative they were. Most of the studies were experiments which, with a few recent exceptions, were carried out in unrealistic settings, using unrealistic, oversimplified stimuli which were of no interest to the subjects. Any conclusions about whether, and at what age, children who have been sexually abused make reliable witnesses must be tentative until the questioning and treatment of real victims is examined and more realistic experiments are carried out which focus on the particular circumstances of such children.

Bearing this limitation in mind, the general implication of the studies reviewed is that children need not be debarred from giving evidence simply on the basis of age. Their individual abilities and circumstances should be considered in deciding whether they would make competent and credible courtroom witnesses and whether they would sustain any psychological damage by so doing. A general legal requirement that children's evidence be corroborated does not appear to be necessary. Moreover, the particular circumstances in which abuse is likely to occur means that other evidence will only rarely exist and will almost never meet current evidentiary standards. Independent adult witnesses are scarce and physical signs of sexual abuse are not always available or reliable. If the distinction between sworn and unsworn testimony and the corroboration requirement are maintained in relation to children's evidence, it may be worth giving further thought to allowing the unsworn testimony of one child to corroborate the testimony of another.

REFERENCES

BENTOVIM, A. and TRANTER, M. (1987) 'The sexual abuse of children and the courts', in Davies, G.M. and Drinkwater, J.M. (eds.) The Child Witness: Do the Courts abuse Children? Issues in Criminological and Legal Psychology, 13. Leicester: British Psychological Society.++

BERLINER, L. and BARBIERI, M.K. (1984) 'The testimony of the child victim of sexual assault', Journal of Social Issues, 40(2), 125–137.

BROWN, A.L. and CAMPIONE, J.C. (1972) 'Recognition memory for perceptually similar pictures in preschool children', Journal of Experimental Psychology, 95, 55–62.

BROWN, A.L. (1975) 'The development of memory: knowing, knowing about knowing, and knowing how to know', in Reese, H.W. (ed.) Advances in Child Development and Behaviour, Volume 10. New York: Academic Press.

BROWN, A.L. (1982) 'Learning and development: the problem of compatibility, access and induction', Human Development, 25,89–115.

CHANCE, J.E. and GOLDSTEIN, A.G (1984) 'Face recognition memory: implications for children's eyewitness testimony', Journal of Social Issues, 40(2), 69–85.

CHI, M.T.H. (1978) 'Knowledge structures and memory development' in Siegler, R.S. (ed) Children's Thinking: What Develops? Hillsdale: Erlbaum.

COHEN, R.L. and HARNICK, M.A. (1980) 'The susceptibility of child witnesses to suggestion', Law and Human Behaviour, 4, 201–210.

COMMITTEE ON SEXUAL OFFENCES AGAINST CHILDREN AND YOUTHS (1984) Sexual Offences Against Children and Youths. Volume 1. Ottawa, Canada: Ministry of Supply and Services.

CONERLY, S. (1986) 'Assessment of suspected child sexual abuse', in MacFarlane, K. *et al.* (eds.) Sexual Abuse of Young Children. London: Holt, Rinehart and Winston.

++ Forthcoming.

CORSINI-MUNT, L. (1982) 'Sexual abuse of children and adolescents', in Schlesinger, B. (ed.) Sexual Abuse of Children. Toronto: University of Toronto Press.

CRIMINAL LAW REVISION COMMITTEE (1972) Report on Evidence. London: HMSO. CMND 4991.

DALE, P.S., LOFTUS, E.F and RATHBUN, L. (1978) 'The influence of the form of the question on the eyewitness testimony of preschool children', Journal of Psycholinguistic Research, 7, 269-277.

DAVIES, G.M. (1980) 'Can memory be educated?', Educational Studies, 6, 155-161.

DAVIES, G.M., FLIN, R. and BAXTER, J. (1986) 'The Child Witness', Howard Journal, 25(2), 81-99.

DAVIES, G.M. and BROWN, L. (1978) 'Recall and organisation in 5 year old children', British Journal of Psychology, 69, 343-349.

DAVIES, G.M and FLIN, R. (1987a) 'The accuracy and suggestibility of child witnesses', in Davies, G.M. and Drinkwater, J.M. (eds.) The Child Witness: Do the Courts abuse Children? Issues in Criminological and Legal Psychology, 13. Leicester: British Psychological Society.++

DAVIES, G.M and FLIN, R. (1987b) 'Children's identification evidence', in Kohnken, G. and Sporer, S.L. (eds.) Identifizierung von Tatverdachtingen: Psychologische Erkenntnisse, Probleme und Perspektiven. Gottingen: C.J. Hogrefe.++

DENT, H.R. (1977) 'Stress as a factor influencing person recognition in identification parades', Bulletin of the British Psychological Society, 30, 339-340.

DENT, H.R. (1982) 'The effects of interviewing strategies on the results of interviews with child witnesses', in Trankell, A. (ed.) Reconstructing the Past. Stockholm, Sweden: P.A. Norstedt and Sons.

DENT, H.R. and STEPHENSON, G.M. (1979a) 'Identification evidence: experimental investigations of factors affecting the reliability of juvenile and adult witnesses' in Farrington, D.P., Hawkins, K. and Lloyd-Bostock, S.(eds.) Psychology, Law and Legal Processes. London: Macmillan.

DENT, H.R. and STEPHENSON, G.M. (1979b) 'An experimental study of the effectiveness of different techniques of questioning child witnesses', British Journal of Social and Clinical Psychology, 18, 41–51.

EYSENCK, M.W and BARON, C.W. (1974) 'Effects of cueing on the recall of categorised word list', Developmental Psychology, 10, 665–666.

FEINMAN, S. and ENTWHISTLE, D.R. (1976) 'Childen's ability to recognise other children's faces', Child Development, 47, 506–510.

FELDMAN, R.S. and WHITE, J.B. (1980) 'Detecting deception in children', Journal of Communication, 30(2), 121–128.

FELDMAN, R.S., JENKINS, L. and POPOOLA, O. (1979) 'Detection of deception in adults and children via facial expressions', Child Development, 50(2), 350–355.

FREUD, S. (1959) 'On the Sexual Theories of Children' in Collected Papers. New York: Basic Books.

GLAZER, D. (1986) Interviewing children who have not been abused with anatomically correct dolls. Paper presented to the Association of Child Psychology and Psychiatry.

GOLDSTEIN, A.G. and CHANCE, J.E.(1964) 'Recognition of children's faces', Child Development, 35, 129–136.

GOODMAN, G.S. (1984) 'Children's testimony in historical perspective', Journal of Social Issues, 40(2), 9–31.

GOODMAN, G.S. and REED, R.S. (1986) 'Age differences in eyewitness testimony', Law and Human Behaviour, 10(4), 317–332.

GOODMAN, G.S., GOLDING, J.M., HEDGESON, V.S., HAITH, M.M. and MICHELLI, J. (1987a) 'When a child takes the stand: jurors' perceptions of children's eyewitness testimony', Law and Human Behaviour, 11(1), 27–40.

GOODMAN, G.S., AMAN, C. and HIRSCHAMN, J. (1987b) 'Child sexual and physical abuse: children's testimony', in Ceci, S.J., Toglia, M.P. and Ross, D.F. Children's Eyewitness Memory. New York: Springer-Verlag.

GOODWIN, J., CAUTHORNE C.G and RADA, R.T (1980) 'Cinderella Syndrome: children who simulate neglect', American Journal of Psychiatry, 137, 1223–1225.

GORENSTEIN, G.W. and ELLSWORTH, P.C. (1980) 'Effect of choosing an incorrect photograph on a later identification by an eyewitness', Journal of Applied Psychology, 65, 612-622.

GUDJONSONN, G. (1983) 'Lie detection: techniques and countermeasures', in Lloyd-Bostock, S.M.A. and Clifford, B.R. (eds.) Evaluating Witness Evidence. Chichester: John Wiley.

GWYNN, P. (1987) 'Investigating child abuse: the Bexley project', in Davies, G.M. and Drinkwater, J.M. (eds.) The Child Witness: Do the Courts abuse Children? Issues in Criminological and Legal Psychology, 13. Leicester: British Psychological Society.++

JABLONSKI, E.M. (1974) 'Free recall in children', Psychological Bulletin, 81(9), 522-539.

JENKINS, F. and DAVIES, G.M. (1985) 'Contamination of facial memory through exposure to misleading composite pictures', Journal of Applied Psychology, 70, 164-175.

JOHNSON, M.K. and FOLEY, M.A. (1984) 'Differentiating fact from fantasy: the reliability of children's memory', Journal of Social Issues, 40(2), 33-50.

JONES, D.P.H. (1987) 'The evidence of a three-year-old child' Criminal Law Review, October, 677-680.

JONES, D.P.H. and McGRAW, J.M. (1987) 'Reliable and fictitious accounts of sexual abuse to children', Journal of Interpersonal Violence, 2(1), 27-45.

KAIL, R. (1985) The development of memory in children. New York: Freeman.

KING, M.A. and YUILLE, J.C. (1987) 'Suggestibility and the child witness' in Ceci, S.J., Toglia, M.P. and Ross, D.F. Children's Eyewitness Memory. New York: Springer-Verlag.

KOHNKEN, G. and STELLER, M. (1987) 'The evaluation of the credibility of child witness statements in the German procedural system', in Davies, G.M. and Drinkwater, J.M. (eds.) The Child Witness: Do the Courts abuse Children? Issues in Criminological and Legal Psychology, 13. Leicester: British Psychological Society.++

KRUGMAN, R. and JONES, D.P.H. (1987) 'Incest and other forms of sexual abuse' in Helfer, R.E. and Kempe R.S. (eds.) The Battered Child. Chicago: University of Chicago Press (4th edition).

LINDSAY, D.S. and JOHNSON, M.K. (1987) 'Reality monitoring and suggestibility: children's ability to discriminate among memories from different sources' in Ceci, S.J., Toglia, M.P. and Ross, D.F. Children's Eyewitness Memory. New York: Springer-Verlag.

LOFTUS, E.F. (1979) Eyewitness Testimony. Cambridge, Mass: Harvard University Press.

LOFTUS, E.F. and DAVIES, G.M. (1984) 'Distortions in the memory of children', Journal of Social Issues, 40(2) 51-67.

LOFTUS, E.F. and GREEN, E. (1980) 'Warning: even memory for faces may be contagious', Law and Human Behaviour, 4, 323-334.

LOFTUS, E.F. and PALMER, J.C. (1974) 'Reconstruction of automobile destruction: an example of the interaction between language and memory', Journal of Verbal Learning and Verbal Behaviour, 13, 585-589.

MALPASS, R.S. and DEVINE, P.G (1981) 'Realism and eyewitness identification research', Law and Human Behaviour, 4(4), 347-358.

MANN, E.M. (1985) 'The assessment of credibility of sexually abused children in criminal court cases', American Journal of Forensic Psychiatry, VI(2), 9-15.

MARIN, B.V., HOLMES, D.L., GUTH, M. and KOVAC,P. (1979) 'The potential of children as eyewitnesses', Law and Human Behaviour, 3(4), 295-305.

McCORD, D. (1986) 'Expert testimony about child complainants in sexual abuse prosecutions: a foray into the admissibility of novel psychological evidence', Journal of Criminal Law and Criminology, 77(1) 1-68.

MELTON, G.B. (1981) 'Children's competency to testify', Law and Human Behaviour, 5(1), 73-85.

MORI (1984) Child Abuse: a research study on behalf of Gamble and Milne. London: Market Opinion and Research Ltd.

NASH, C.L. and WEST, D.J. (1985) 'Sexual molestation of young girls' in West, D.J. (ed.) Sexual Victimisation. London: Gower.

NELSON, K. (1978) 'How young children represent knowledge of their world in and out of language',in Siegler, R.S. (ed) Children's Thinking: What Develops? Hillsdale: Erlbaum.

ORNSTEIN, P. (1978) Memory Development in Children. New Jersey: Lawrence Erlbaum Associates.

PARKER, J.F., HAVERFIELD, E. and BAKER-THOMAS, S. (1986) 'Eyewitness testimony of children', Journal of Applied Social Psychology, 16, 287-302.

PETERS, D.P. (1987) 'The impact of naturally occurring stress on children's memory' in Ceci, S.J., Toglia, M.P. and Ross, D.F. Children's Eyewitness Memory. New York: Springer-Verlag.

PYNOOS, R.S. and ETH, S. (1984) 'The child as witness to homicide', Journal of Social Issues, 40(2), 87- 108.

RABINOWITZ, M.J. (1985) 'The child as eyewitness: an overview', Social Action and the Law, 11(1), 5-10.

ROSENFELD, A.A., NADELSON, C.C. and KRIEGER, M. (1979) 'Fantasy and reality in patients reports of incest', Journal of Clinical Psychiatry, 40, 159-164.

ROSS, D.F., MILLER, B.S. and MORAN, P.B. (1987) 'The child in the eyes of the jury: assessing mock jurors' perceptions of the child witness'in Ceci, S.J., Toglia, M.P. and Ross, D.F. Children's Eyewitness Memory. New York: Springer-Verlag.

SPENCER, J.R. (1987) 'Child witnesses, corroboration and expert evidence', Criminal Law Review, April, 239-251.

STERN, L.W. (1910) 'Abstracts of lectures on the psychology of testimony on the study of individuality', American Journal of Psychology, 21, 270-282.

TSCHIRGI, J.E. (1980) 'Sensible reasoning: a hypothesis about hypotheses', Child Development, 51, 1-10.

TULVING, E. (1983) Elements of Episodic Memory. Oxford: Oxford University Press.

UNDEUTSCH, U. (1982) 'Statement Reality Analysis', in Trankell, A. (ed.) Reconstructing the Past. Stockholm, Sweden: P.A. Norstedt and Sons.

WEINBERG, H.I., WADSWORTH, J. and BARON, R.S. (1983) 'Demand and the impact of leading questions on eyewitness testimony', Memory and Cognition, 11, 101-104.

WEISS, E. (1983) 'Incest accusation: assessing credibility', Journal of Psychiatry and Law, Fall, 305-317.

YARMEY, A.D (1984) 'Age as a factor in eyewitness memory', in Wells, G. and Loftus, E.F. (eds.) Eyewitness testimony: psychological perspectives. New York: Cambridge University Press.

YUILLE, J.C., CUTSHALL, J.L and KING, M.A. (1986) 'Age related changes in eyewitness accounts and photo-identification', (unpublished).

Reports published in the SCDTO and HORS series are available from HMSO who will advise as to prices (Tel. 01 622 3316). Those marked with an asterisk are out of print, but photostat copies are still available. Reports published in the RUP and RPUP series are available from the Home Office Research and Planning Unit, Information Section, 50 Queen Anne's Gate, London, SW1H 9AT.

Studies in the Causes of Delinquency and the Treatment of Offenders (SCDTO)

1. Prediction methods in relation to borstal training. Hermann Mannheim and Leslie T. Wilkins. 1955. viii + 276pp. (11 340051 9).

2. *Time spent awaiting trial. Evelyn Gibson. 1960. v + 45pp. (34-368-2).

3. *Delinquent generations. Leslie T. Wilkins. 1960. iv + 20pp. (11 340053 5).

4. *Murder. Evelyn Gibson and S. Klein. 1961. iv + 44pp. (11 340054 3).

5. Persistent criminals. A study of all offenders liable to preventive detention in 1956. W.H. Hammond and Edna Chayen. 1963. ix + 237pp. (34-368-5).

6. *Some statistical and other numerical techniques for classifying individuals. P. McNaughton-Smith. 1965. v + 33pp. (34-368-6).

7. Probation research: a preliminary report. Part I. General outline of research. Part II. Study of Middlesex probation area (SOMPA). Steven Folkard, Kate Lyon, Margaret M. Carver and Erica O'Leary. 1966. vi + 58pp. (11 340374 7).

8. *Probation research: national study of probation. Trends and regional comparisons in probation (England and Wales). Hugh Barr and Erica O'Leary. 1966. vii + 51pp. (34-368-8).

9. *Probation research. A survey of group work in the probation service. Hugh Barr. 1966. vii + 94pp. (34-368-9).

10. *Types of delinquency and home background. A validation study of Hewitt and Jenkins' hypothesis. Elizabeth Field. 1967. vi + 21pp. (34-368-10).

11. *Studies of female offenders. No. 1 - Girls of 16-20 years sentenced to borstal or detention centre training in 1963. No. 2 - Women offenders in the Metropolitan Police District in March and April 1957. No. 3 - A description of women in prison on January 1, 1965. Nancy Goodman and Jean Price. 1967. v + 78pp. (34-368-11).

12. *The use of the Jesness Inventory on a sample of British probationers. Martin Davies. 1967. iv + 20pp. (34-368-12).

13. *The Jesness Inventory: application to approved school boys. Joy Mott. 1969. iv + 27pp. (11 340063 2).

Home Office Research Studies (HORS)

1. *Workloads in children's departments. Eleanor Grey. 1969. vi + 75pp. (11 340101 9).

2. *Probationers in their social environment. A study of male probationers aged 17-20, together with an analysis of those reconvicted within twelve months. Martin Davies. 1969. vii + 204pp. (11 340102 7).

3. *Murder 1957 to 1968. A Home Office Statistical Division report on murder in England and Wales. Evelyn Gibson and S. Klein (with annex by the Scottish Home and Health Department on murder in Scotland). 1969. vi + 94pp. (11 340103 5).

4. Firearms in crime. A Home Office Statistical Division report on indictable offences involving firearms in England and Wales. A. D. Weatherhead and B. M. Robinson. 1970. viii + 39pp. (11 340104 3).

5. *Financial penalties and probation. Martin Davies. 1970. vii + 39pp. (11 340105 1).

6. *Hostels for probationers. A study of the aims, working and variations in effectiveness of male probation hostels with special reference to the influence of the environment on delinquency. Ian Sinclair. 1971. ix + 200pp. (11 340106 X).

7. *Prediction methods in criminology – including a prediction study of young men on probation. Frances H. Simon. 1971. xi + 234pp. (11 340107 8).

8. *Study of the juvenile liaison scheme in West Ham 1961-65. Marilyn Taylor. 1971. vi + 46pp. (11 340108 6).

9. *Explorations in after-care. I – After-care units in London, Liverpool and Manchester. Martin Silberman (Royal London Prisoners' Aid Society) and Brenda Chapman. II – After-care hostels receiving a Home Office grant. Ian Sinclair and David Snow (HORU). III – St. Martin of Tours House, Aryeh Leissner (National Bureau for Co-operation in Child Care). 1971. xi + 140pp. (11 340109 4).

10. A survey of adoption in Great Britain. Eleanor Grey in collaboration with Ronald M. Blunden. 1971. ix + 168pp. (11 340110 8).

11. *Thirteen-year-old approved school boys in 1962s. Elizabeth Field, W. H. Hammond and J. Tizard. 1971. ix + 46pp. (11 340111 6).

12. Absconding from approved schools. R. V. G. Clarke and D. N. Martin.

1971. vi + 146pp. (11 340112 4).

13. An experiment in personality assessment of young men remanded in custody. H. Sylvia Anthony. 1972. viii + 79pp. (11 340113 2).

14. *Girl offenders aged 17–20 years. I – Statistics relating to girl offenders aged 17–20 years from 1960 to 1970. II – Re-offending by girls released from borstal or detention centre training. III – The problems of girls released from borstal training during their period on after-care. Jean Davies and Nancy Goodman. 1972. v + 77pp. (11 340114 0).

15. *The controlled trial in institutional research – paradigm or pitfall for penal evaluators? R. V. G. Clarke and D. B. Cornish. 1972. v + 33pp. (11 340115 9).

16. *A survey of fine enforcement. Paul Softley. 1973. v + 65pp. (11 340116 7).

17. *An index of social environment – designed for use in social work
 menum   research. Martin Davies. 1973. vi + 63pp. (11 340117 5).

18. *Social enquiry reports and the probation service. Martin Davies and Andrea Knopf. 1973. v + 49pp. (11 340118 3).

19. *Depression, psychopathic personality and attempted suicide in a borstal sample. H. Sylvia Anthony. 1973. viii + 44pp. (0 11 340119 1).

20. *The use of bail and custody by London magistrates' courts before and after the Criminal Justice Act 1967. Frances Simon and Mollie Weatheritt. 1974. vi + 78pp. (0 11 340120 5).

21. *Social work in the environment. A study of one aspect of probation practice. Martin Davies, with Margaret Rayfield, Alaster Calder and Tony Fowles. 1974. ix + 151pp. (0 11 340121 3).

22. Social work in prison. An experiment in the use of extended contact with offenders. Margaret Shaw. 1974. viii + 154pp. (0 11 340122 1).

23. Delinquency amongst opiate users. Joy Mott and Marilyn Taylor. 1974. vi + 31pp. (0 11 340663 0).

24. IMPACT. Intensive matched probation and after-care treatment. Vol. I – The design of the probation experiment and an interim evaluation. M. S. Folkard, A. J. Fowles, B.C. McWilliams, W. McWilliams, D. D. Smith, D. E. Smith and G. R. Walmsley. 1974. v + 54pp. (0 11 340664 9).

25. The approved school experience. An account of boys' experiences of training under differing regimes of approved schools, with an attempt to evaluate the effectiveness of that training. Anne B. Dunlop. 1974. vii + 124pp. (0 11 340665 7).

26. *Absconding from open prisons. Charlotte Banks, Patricia Mayhew and R. J. Sapsford. 1975. viii + 89pp. (0 11 340666 5).

27. Driving while disqualified. Sue Kriefman. 1975. vi + 136pp.
    (0 11 340667 3).

28. Some male offenders' problems. I - Homeless offenders in Liverpool. W.
    McWilliams. II - Casework with short-term prisoners. Julie Holborn.
    1975. x + 147pp. (0 11 340668 1).

29. *Community service orders. K. Pease, P. Durkin, I. Earnshaw, D. Payne
    and J. Thorpe. 1975. viii + 80pp. (0 11 340669 X).

30. Field Wing Bail Hostel: the first nine months. Frances Simon and Sheena
    Wilson. 1975. viii + 55pp. (0 11 340670 3).

31. Homicide in England and Wales 1967-1971. Evelyn Gibson. 1975.
    iv + 59pp. (0 11 340753 X).

32. Residential treatment and its effects on delinquency. D. B. Cornish and
    R. V. G. Clarke. 1975. vi + 74pp. (0 11 340672 X).

33. Further studies of female offenders. Part A: Borstal girls eight years
    after release. Nancy Goodman, Elizabeth Maloney and Jean Davies.
    Part B: The sentencing of women at the London Higher Courts. Nancy
    Goodman, Paul Durkin and Janet Halton. Part C: Girls appearing before
    a juvenile court. Jean Davies. 1976. vi + 114pp. (0 11 340673 8).

34. *Crime as opportunity. P. Mayhew, R. V. G. Clarke, A. Sturman and J. M.
    Hough. 1976. vii + 36pp. (0 11 340674 6).

35. The effectiveness of sentencing: a review of the literature. S. R.
    Brody. 1976. v + 89pp. (0 11 340675 4).

36. IMPACT. Intensive matched probation and after-care treatment. Vol. II -
    The results of the experiment. M. S. Folkard, D. E. Smith and D. D.
    1976. xi + 40pp. (0 11 340676 2).

37. Police cautioning in England and Wales. J. A. Ditchfield. 1976.
    v + 31pp. (0 11 340677 0).

38. Parole in England and Wales. C. P. Nuttall, with E. E. Barnard, A. J.
    Fowles, A. Frost, W. H. Hammond, P. Mayhew, K. Pease, R. Tarling and
    M. J. Weatheritt. 1977. vi +
    90pp. (0 11 340678 9).

39. Community service assessed in 1976. K. Pease, S. Billingham and I.
    Earnshaw. 1977. vi + 29pp. (0 11 340679 7).

40. Screen violence and film censorship:a review of research. Stephen Brody.
    1977. vii + 179pp. (0 11 340680 0).

41. *Absconding from borstals. Gloria K. Laycock. 1977. v + 82pp.
    (0 11 340681 9).

42. Gambling: a review of the literature and its implications for policy and research. D. B. Cornish. 1978. xii + 284pp. (0 11 340682 7).

43. Compensation orders in magistrates' courts. Paul Softley. 1978. v + 41pp. (0 11 340683 5).

44. Research in criminal justice. John Croft. 1978. iv + 16pp. (0 11 340684 3).

45. Prison welfare: an account of an experiment at Liverpool. A. J. Fowles. 1978. v + 34pp. (0 11 340685 1).

46. Fines in magistrates' courts. Paul Softley. 1978. v + 42pp. (0 11 340686 X).

47. Tackling vandalism. R. V. G. Clarke (editor), F. J. Gladstone, A. Sturman and Sheena Wilson (contributors). 1978. vi + 91pp. (0 11 340687 8).

48. Social inquiry reports: a survey. Jennifer Thorpe. 1979. vi + 55pp. (0 11 340688 6).

49. Crime in public view. P. Mayhew, R. V. G. Clarke, J. N. Burrows, J. M. Hough and S. W. C. Winchester. 1979. v + 36pp. (0 11 340689 4).

50. *Crime and the community. John Croft. 1979. v + 16pp. (0 11 340690 8).

51. Life-sentence prisoners. David Smith (editor), Christopher Brown, Joan Worth, Roger Sapsford and Charlotte Banks (contributors). 1979. iv + 51pp. (0 11 340691 6).

52. Hostels for offenders. Jane E. Andrews, with an appendix by Bill Sheppard. 1979. v + 30pp. (0 11 340692 4).

53. Previous convictions, sentence and reconviction: a statistical study of a sample of 5,000 offenders convicted in January 1971. G. J. O. Phillpotts and L. B. Lancucki. 1979. v + 55pp. (0 11 340693 2).

54. Sexual offences, consent and sentencing. Roy Walmsley and Karen White. 1979. vi + 77pp. (0 11 340694 0).

55. Crime prevention and the police. John Burrows, Paul Ekblom and Kevin Heal. 1979. v + 37pp. (0 11 340695 9).

56. Sentencing practice in magistrates' courts. Roger Tarling, with the assistance of Mollie Weatheritt. 1979. vii + 54pp. (0 11 340696 7).

57. Crime and comparative research. John Croft. 1979. iv + 16pp. (0 11 340697 5).

58. Race, crime and arrests. Philip Stevens and Carole F. Willis. 1979. v + 69pp. (0 11 340698 3).

59. Research and criminal policy. John Croft. 1980. iv + 14pp.
(0 11 340699 1).

60. Junior attendance centres. Anne B. Dunlop. 1980. v + 47pp.
(0 11 340700 9).

61. Police interrogation: an observational study in four police stations.
Paul Softley, with the assistance of David Brown, Bob Forde, George Mair
and David Moxon. 1980. vii + 67pp. (0 11 340701 7).

62. Co-ordinating crime prevention efforts. F. J. Gladstone. 1980.
v + 74pp. (0 11 340702 5).

63. Crime prevention publicity: an assessment. D. Riley and P. Mayhew.
1980. v + 47pp. (0 11 340703 3).

64. Taking offenders out of circulation. Stephen Brody and Roger Tarling.
1980. v + 46pp. (0 11 340704 1).

65. *Alcoholism and social policy: are we on the right lines? Mary Tuck.
1980. v + 30pp. (0 11 340705 X).

66. Persistent petty offenders. Suzan Fairhead. 1981. vi + 78pp.
(0 11 340706 8).

67. Crime control and the police. Pauline Morris and Kevin Heal. 1981.
v + 71pp. (0 11 340707 6).

68. Ethnic minorities in Britain: a study of trends in their position since
1961. Simon Field, George Mair, Tom Rees and Philip Stevens. 1981.
v + 48pp. (0 11 340708 4).

69. Managing criminological research. John Croft. 1981. iv + 17pp.
(0 11 340709 2).

70. Ethnic minorities, crime and policing: a survey of the experiences of
West Indians and whites. Mary Tuck and Peter Southgate. 1981. iv + 54pp.
(0 11 340765 3).

71. Contested trials in magistrates' courts. Julie Vennard. 1982.
v + 32pp. (0 11 340766 1).

72. Public disorder: a review of research and a study in one inner city
area. Simon Field and Peter Southgate. 1982. v + 77pp.
(0 11 340767 X).

73. Clearing up crime. John Burrows and Roger Tarling. 1982. vii + 31pp.
(0 11 340768 8).

74. Residential burglary: the limits of prevention. Stuart Winchester and
Hilary Jackson. 1982. v + 47pp. (0 11 340769 6).

75. Concerning crime. John Croft. 1982. iv + 16pp. (0 11 340770 X).

76. The British Crime Survey: first report. Mike Hough and Pat Mayhew. 1983. v + 62pp. (0 11 340786 6).

77. Contacts between police and public: findings from the British Crime Survey. Peter Southgate and Paul Ekblom. 1984. v + 42pp. (0 11 340771 8).

78. Fear of crime in England and Wales. Michael Maxfield. 1984. v + 57pp. (0 11 340772 6).

79. Crime and police effectiveness. Ronald V Clarke and Mike Hough 1984. iv + 33pp. (0 11 340773 3).

80. The attitudes of ethnic minorities. Simon Field. 1984. v + 49pp. (0 11 340774 2).

81. Victims of crime: the dimensions of risk. Michael Gottfredson.1984. v + 54pp.(0 11 340775 0).

82. The tape recording of police interviews with suspects: an interim report. Carole Willis.1984.v + 45pp.(0 11 340776 9).

83. Parental supervision and juvenile delinquency. David Riley and Margaret Shaw. 1985.v + 90pp.(0 11 340799 8).

84. Adult prisons and prisoners in England and Wales 1970-1982: a review of the findings of social research. Joy Mott. 1985. vi + 73pp.(0 11 340801 3).

85. Taking account of crime: key findings from the 1984 British Crime Survey. Mike Hough and Pat Mayhew. 1985. vi + 115pp. (0 11 341810 2).

86. Implementing crime prevention measures. Tim Hope. 1985. vi + 82pp.(0 11 340812 9).

87. Resettling refugees: the lessons of research. Simon Field. 1985. vi + 66pp.(0 11 340815 3).

88. Investigating burglary: the measurement of police performance. John Burrows. 1986. vi + 36pp. (0 11 340824 2).

89. Personal violence. Roy Walmsley. 1986. vi + 87pp. (0 11 340827 7).

90. Police-public encounters. Peter Southgate. 1986. vi + 150pp.

91. Grievance procedures in prisons. John Ditchfield and Claire Austin. 1986. vi + 78pp. (0 11 340839 0).

92. The effectiveness of the Forensic Science Service. Malcolm Ramsay.1987. v + 100pp. (0 11 340842 0).

93. The police complaints procedure: a survey of complaint's views. David Brown. 1987. v + 98pp. (0 11 340853 6).

94. The validity of the reconviction prediction score. Denis Ward. 1987. vi + 46pp. (0 11 340882 X).

ALSO

Designing out crime. R. V. G. Clarke and P. Mayhew (editors). 1980. viii + 186pp. (0 11 340732 7).
(This book collects, with an introduction, studies that were originally published in HORS 34, 47, 49, 55, 62 and 63 and which are illustrative of the 'situational' approach to crime prevention.)

Policing today. Kevin Heal, Roger Tarling and John Burrows (editors). v + 181pp. (0 11 340800 5).
(This book brings together twelve separate studies on police matters produced during the last few years by the Unit.The collection records some relatively little known contributions to the debate on policing.)

Managing Criminal Justice: a collection of papers. David Moxon (editor). 1985. vi + 222pp. (0 11 340811 0).
(This book brings together a number of studies bearing on the management of the criminal justice system. It includes papers by social scientists and operational researchers working within the Research and Planning Unit, and academic researchers who have studied particular aspects of the criminal process.)

Situational Crime Prevention: from theory into practice. Kevin Heal and Gloria Laycock (editors). 1986. vii + 166pp. (0 11 340826 9).
(This book is a collection of essays on theoretical, practical and policy issues in crime prevention.

Research Unit Papers (RUP)

1. Uniformed police work and management technology. J. M. Hough. 1980.

2. Supplementary information on sexual offences and sentencing. Roy Walmsley and Karen White. 1980.

3. Board of visitor adjudications. David Smith, Claire Austin and John Ditchfield. 1981.

4. Day centres and probation. Suzan Fairhead, with the assistance of J. Wilkinson-Grey. 1981.

Research and Planning Unit Papers (RPUP)

5. Ethnic minorities and complaints against the police. Philip Stevens and Carole Willis. 1982.

6. * Crime and public housing. Mike Hough and Pat Mayhew (editors). 1982.

7. * Abstracts of race relations research. George Mair and Philip Stevens (editors). 1982.

8. Police probationer training in race relations. Peter Southgate. 1982.

9. * The police response to calls from the public. Paul Ekblom and Kevin Heal. 1982.

10. City centre crime: a situational approach to prevention. Malcolm Ramsay. 1982.

11. Burglary in schools: the prospects for prevention. Tim Hope. 1982.

12.* Fine enforcement. Paul Softley and David Moxon. 1982.

13. Vietnamese refugees. Peter Jones. 1982.

14. Community resources for victims of crime. Karen Williams. 1983.

15. The use, effectiveness and impact of police stop and search powers. Carole Willis. 1983.

16. Acquittal rates. Sid Butler. 1983.

17. Criminal justice comparisons: the case of Scotland and England and Wales. Lorna J. F. Smith. 1983.

18. Time taken to deal with juveniles under criminal proceedings. Catherine Frankenburg and Roger Tarling. 1983.

19. Civilian review of complaints against the police: a survey of the

United States literature. David C. Brown. 1983.

20. Police action on motoring offences. David Riley. 1983.

21.* Diverting drunks from the criminal justice system. Sue Kingsley and
     George Mair. 1983.

22. The staff resource implications of an independent prosecution system.
     Peter R. Jones. 1983

23. Reducing the prison population: an exploratory study in Hampshire.
     David Smith, Bill Sheppard, George Mair, Karen Williams. 1984.

24. Criminal justice system model: magistrates' courts sub-model.
     Susan Rice. 1984.

25. Measures of police effectiveness and efficiency. Ian Sinclair
     and Clive Miller. 1984.

26. Punishment practice by prison Boards of Visitors. Susan Iles,
     Adrienne Connors, Chris May, Joy Mott. 1984.

27.* Reparation,conciliation and mediation:current projects and
     plans in England and Wales. Tony Marshall. 1984.

28. Magistrates' domestic courts:new perspectives. Tony Marshall
     (editor). 1984.

29. Racism awareness training for the police. Peter Southgate.
     1984.

30. Community constables:a study of a policing initiative. David
     Brown and Susan Iles. 1985.

31. Recruiting volunteers. Hilary Jackson. 1985.

32. Juvenile sentencing:is there a tariff? David Moxon,Peter Jones,
     Roger Tarling. 1985.

33. Bringing people together:mediation and reparation projects in Great
     Britain. Tony Marshall and Martin Walpole. 1985.

34. Remands in the absence of the accused. Chris May. 1985.

35. Modelling the criminal justice system. Patricia M Morgan. 1985.

36. The criminal justice system model: the flow model. Hugh Pullinger. 1986.

37. Burglary: police actions and victim views. John Burrows. 1986.

38. Unlocking community resources: four experimental government small
     grants schemes. Hilary Jackson. 1986.

39. The Cost of Discriminating: a review of the Literature. Shirley Dex. 1986.

40. Waiting for crown court trial: the remand population. Rachel Pearce.1987.